my body belongs to me

A book about body safety

Jill Starishevsky

Illustrated by Angela Padrón

free spirit
PUBLISHING®

Text copyright © 2014 by Jill Starishevsky
Illustrations copyright © 2014 by Angela Padrón
A previous edition of this book was published by Safety Star Media in 2008.

Library of Congress Cataloging-in-Publication
Control Number: 2013050393

eBook: 978-1-57542-594-8

Free Spirit Publishing does not have control over or assume responsibility for author or third-party websites and their content. At the time of this book's publication, all telephone numbers and website URLs are accurate and active. If you find an error or believe that a resource listed here is not as described, please contact Free Spirit Publishing.

Reading Level Grade 1; Interest Level Ages 3–8;
Fountas & Pinnell Guided Reading Level J

Edited by Alison Behnke

10 9 8 7 6 5 4 3 2 1
Printed in China
R18860114

Free Spirit Publishing Inc.
Minneapolis, MN
(612) 338-2068
help4kids@freespirit.com
www.freespirit.com

Free Spirit offers competitive pricing.
Contact edsales@freespirit.com for pricing information on multiple quantity purchases.

QBI 6/14 $12.99

For Ted, Ally, Becca, and Emma,
the loves of my life. And for T.T.,
whose courage beyond her years
became my inspiration.

Acknowledgments

Special thanks to Robert T. Johnson, Bronx County District Attorney, who has given me the opportunity to do the job I love, and to Elisa Koenderman and Joseph Muroff, former and current chiefs of the Bronx County District Attorney's Child Abuse and Sex Crimes Bureau, respectively, whose guidance and support have been instrumental in my development as a prosecutor.

Thanks also to Pamela Pine from Stop the Silence, for her wealth of information about child sexual abuse. And of course, thanks to my family for their feedback and constant support, and to my husband and biggest fan, Ted, who is my collaborator and partner in all ways, and is forever helping me multitask.

A Letter to Grown-Ups

Among the first things we teach children is to name the various parts of their bodies. As they grow older, this conversation should go a step further: Some parts of their bodies are private and belong just to them.

Just as we teach young people what to do in case of fire, we must teach them what to do if someone touches them inappropriately—or forces them to touch others inappropriately. The central message of *My Body Belongs to Me* is this: If someone touches you, *tell*.

Unfortunately, the overwhelming majority of sexually abused children *don't* immediately disclose the abuse. As a result, the abuse can often grow more serious. There are many reasons for a child's silence. Perhaps the abuser says it's a secret. Maybe the child believes that he or she is at fault. Without being taught that his or her body has boundaries, a child may be too young to understand that the behavior is wrong.

Any child—regardless of gender, age, or background—may become a victim of abuse. Yet adults often don't know how or when to approach this topic with young children. Written for 3- to 8-year-olds, *My Body Belongs to Me* can help you start this difficult discussion and talk about body boundaries and safety with children in a straightforward, sensitive way.

Jill

P.S. On pages 24–26, you'll find suggestions for sharing this book with children. And on pages 26–27, you'll see a list of other sources of help and information.

This is my body,
and it belongs just to me.

I have **knees**
and
elbows
and lots of parts you see.

Other parts I have
are not in open view.

I call them my private parts.
Of course, you have them too.

5

Mom and Dad once told me
I was their little gem,

and if someone hurt me
to always come to them.

One day when we were visiting my Uncle Johnny's house,

I was playing with some toys,
quiet as a mouse.

My uncle's friend came over
and sat down next to me,

and touched me
in that place
that no one else can see.

12

I got so scared I froze
and just stayed where I sat.

I thought:

This is **MY** body!

Why did he do that?

He said it was our secret
and told me not to tell.

But I ran away real fast,
and then began to yell.

I told my mom and dad
what had taken place.

They said that I was really brave
and then each kissed my face.

Mom and Dad said they were proud
I told them right away.

It made me feel better, too—
they believed what I had to say.

I learned if I was too scared
to tell my mom or dad,

I could have told my teacher
what made me feel so sad.

I know it wasn't my fault
and I did nothing wrong.

This is my body,
and I'm growing
big and strong.

Suggestions for Sharing This Book with Children

The following are some tips for using *My Body Belongs to Me* with children.

1. **Use the story as a tool** to begin a conversation. Address the topic periodically to reinforce the message.

2. **Teach children the correct terms for their body parts.** Enable them to use language that will make them comfortable talking to you.

3. **Help children understand that their bodies have boundaries** and no one else has the right to cross those boundaries. Ask: What would you do if someone touched you on your _____? What if someone made you touch his or her _____? Who would you tell? Why is it important to tell? What would you do if the person said it was a secret?

   Encourage children to say that they should and would tell a trusted adult—whether that be a parent, a teacher, or another grown-up—right away.

4. **Discuss the importance of the rule "no secrets."** If you are using this book with your own children or with children in your family, put this rule into practice: If someone, even a grandparent, says something to the child like, "I'll get you an ice cream later, but it will be our secret," firmly but politely say, "We don't do secrets in our family." Then turn to the child and repeat, "We don't do secrets. We can tell each other everything."

5. **Be aware and open.** Keep in mind, especially when reading the book in a group setting, that you may be reading to a child who has already been touched in some way and is keeping it a secret. Convey that it is okay for the child to tell someone even if he or she has been keeping it a secret for a long time.

6. **Know the guidelines.** If you are using the book in an educational or counseling setting, be sure you have an understanding of how to respond if a child makes a disclosure. Every state has mandatory reporting laws that require teachers, counselors, and other professionals to make an immediate report when they learn of abusive situations. Several states have passed laws requiring schools to teach kids about sexual abuse prevention.

7. **Be sure not to respond to a disclosure with anger,** whether you are a

parent, teacher, caregiver, or other adult working with children, Children will often confuse anger toward the perpetrator with anger at them, which can then make them afraid to tell adults about abuse. If a child does make a disclosure, it is important to take it seriously and promptly report it to the appropriate authorities.

8. **Help each child identify a "safety zone person."** A safety zone person can be a teacher, a neighbor, a counselor, a family friend, a figure in the child's faith community, or anyone the child trusts and feels comfortable confiding in. Teach children that if they feel unable, unwilling, or afraid to tell a parent about behavior that made them feel uncomfortable, they should tell their safety zone person. Children can also go to this person for help with other challenging issues, such as bullying. Ideally, the safety zone person should be advised that they have been chosen and should be instructed to discuss any red-flag situations with the child's parents or caregivers in a timely manner.

9. **Keep in mind that child predators often try to entice or intrigue children** they target by offering something inappropriate, such as letting them watch an adult movie, miss school, smoke a cigarette, or drink alcohol.

Children will often be reluctant to tell about inappropriate touching for fear they will get in trouble for the forbidden behavior. Explain to children that if someone touches them inappropriately, they should tell a parent or safety zone person, even if they did something that they were not allowed to do. Similarly, if you are sharing this book with children in your own family, teach them that they can come to you to discuss anything, even if they are worried about getting in trouble. Convey to them that you will listen with an open mind, even if they were doing something they should not have been doing.

10. **Encourage children to tell you or other adults about things that happen to them** that make them feel scared, sad, or uncomfortable. If children have an open line of communication, they will be more inclined to alert you to something inappropriate early on.

11. **Let children decide for themselves how they want to express affection.** Children should not be forced to hug or kiss if it makes them feel uncomfortable. Allowing children to set these boundaries regarding physical contact will empower them to say no to inappropriate touching.

12. **Encourage children to trust their feelings.** If something doesn't feel right, they should get away as soon as possible and tell someone about it.

Revisit these suggestions regularly to help you introduce and explore this important topic with young children. We can teach children about water safety without making them fearful of water. We need to do the same when it comes to keeping their bodies safe. By following these steps, together we can help break the cycle of child abuse.

Where to Find Help and Information

Childhelp
1-800-4-A-CHILD
www.childhelp.org
Childhelp is a national nonprofit organization with a mission to helping victims of child abuse and neglect, with a focus on prevention, intervention, and treatment. Childhelp runs the National Child Abuse Hotline, which operates 24 hours a day, 7 days a week.

Darkness to Light
1-866-FOR-LIGHT
www.D2L.org
Darkness to Light's mission is to shift responsibility for preventing child sexual abuse from children to adults by providing information on how to prevent, recognize, and react responsibly to child sexual abuse.

Jacob Wetterling Resource Center (JWRC)
1-800-325-HOPE
www.jwrc.org
JWRC's mission is to educate families and communities and prevent the exploitation of children. JWRC provides resources, support, and education to ensure every child grows up in a healthy, safe world free from exploitation and abduction.

National Center for Missing & Exploited Children (NCMEC)
1-800-THE-LOST
www.missingkids.com
NCMEC is a public-private partnership serving as a national clearinghouse for information on missing children and the prevention of child victimization. NCMEC works in conjunction with the U.S. Department of Justice's Office of Juvenile Justice and Delinquency Prevention.

RAINN

1-800-656-HOPE

www.rainn.org

RAINN (Rape, Abuse & Incest National Network) is the nation's largest anti-sexual assault organization. RAINN created the National Sexual Assault Hotline, which it operates in partnership with more than 1,100 local rape crisis centers across the country. RAINN also carries out programs to prevent sexual assault, help victims, and ensure that rapists are brought to justice.

Stop It Now!

1-888-PREVENT

www.stopitnow.org

Stop It Now! offers adults the tools they need to prevent sexual abuse before a child is harmed. They provide support, information, and resources that enable individuals and families to keep children safe and create healthier communities. In collaboration with a network of community-based programs, they reach out to adults who are concerned about their own or others' sexualized behavior toward children.

Stop the Silence: Stop Child Sexual Abuse

www.stopcsa.org

Stop the Silence works with others toward the prevention and treatment of child sexual abuse. The worldwide mission of Stop the Silence is to expose and stop child abuse, help survivors heal, and celebrate the lives of those healed.

27

About the Author

Jill Starishevsky has been an assistant district attorney in New York City since 1997, where she has prosecuted thousands of sex offenders and dedicated her career to seeking justice for victims of child abuse and sex crimes. Her mission to protect children, along with her love of poetry, inspired *My Body Belongs to Me*. A mother of three, Jill has been featured on *The Oprah Winfrey Show* and is also a prevention specialist who teaches how to recognize and prevent child sexual abuse. Her website is **mybodybelongstome.com**. Jill lives in New York City.

About the Illustrator

Angela Padrón is a writer and illustrator of children's books and educational material. She earned her M.F.A. in illustration from Academy of Art University, and she also works as an adjunct professor. Angela enjoys spending time in her studio creating works of art using batik, watercolor, pastels, and charcoal, or relaxing at the beach with her family. She lives in Pembroke Pines, Florida.

Other Great Books from Free Spirit

For pricing information, to place an order, or to request a free catalog, contact:

Free Spirit Publishing Inc. • 217 Fifth Avenue North • Suite 200 • Minneapolis, MN 55401-1299
toll-free 800.735.7323 • local 612.338.2068 • fax 612.337.5050 • help4kids@freespirit.com • www.freespirit.com